SAVEONE

A guide to emotional healing
after abortion

Sheila Harper

New York

Paperback ISBN: 978-16003-7437-1

Hardcover ISBN: 978-16003-7438-8

Unless otherwise noted, all Scripture quotations are taken from the New Living Translation (NLT), copyright 1996, Tyndale House Publishers, Inc.

Printed in the United States of America
1 2 3 4 5 6 — 12 11 10 09 08

Published by:

MORGAN · JAMES
THE ENTREPRENEURIAL PUBLISHER
www.morganjamespublishing.com

Morgan James Publishing, LLC
1225 Franklin Ave. Ste 325
Garden City, NY 11530-1693
Toll Free 800-485-4943
www.MorganJamesPublishing.com

Cover design by Diana Lawrence
Page design by Mike Towle

To the woman reading this book: Your courage to come forward and deal with the pain of your abortion astounds me.

Contents

Read First   vii
Acknowledgments   ix
Foreword   x
Introduction   xi

1.   Your Source of Courage   1

2.   What Happened to Me?   17

3.   Dealing with Stray Emotions: Part I   35

4.   Dealing with Stray Emotions: Part II   53

5.   Forgiving Others   67

6.   God's Grace   81

7.   Can I Forgive Myself?   93

8.   Renewing Your Mind   105

9.   Who Is This Child?   119

10. A Woman of Courage   131

In Conclusion   146

Read First

This is a very personal journey for you, and we want to help you through it. If you picked up this book at your local bookstore to complete on your own, we want you to know we would love the chance to travel this journey with you. Please contact the SaveOne staff, and we will confidentially complete this study by your side.

If you are exploring this book to decide if you would like to teach this study at your church or pregnancy center, we would love to talk to you. We have a free Web page to offer you if you become one of our chapters. That way, those who are hurting and come to our site will find the information to contact you directly. We are here to help you help others.

www.saveone.org
866-329-3571
info@saveone.org

Acknowledgments

I would like to acknowledge the people who helped make this book possible. First of all, to my Lord and savior Jesus Christ, thank you for paying the price for my sins. Thank you for saving me, restoring me, and using me as a vessel to bring your restoration to others.

Thank you to my husband, Jack, who did not mind the countless mornings that started at 4:30 A.M. Thanks for being such a wonderful editor. I love you.

Thanks to Pastor Maury Davis for being such a wonderful spiritual authority and mentor in my life. You have helped and furthered the cause of SaveOne more than you will ever know.

Thanks to Donna for sticking by me and for being such an important part of SaveOne.

Thanks to Mike Towle, Judy Petty, and Diana Lawrence. I couldn't have completed this book without your expertise.

Thanks to my BFFs: While dealing with such a heavy subject, you guys provided my comic relief.

Foreword

Every now and then you meet someone whose life precedes them. When Sheila Harper came to me with a personal burden to minister to those precious women who have been involved in a situation that ended with an aborted child, I had no insight into just how far-reaching and needed this ministry would be.

The ministry of SaveOne has, literally, exploded amongst our women. When we first offered the class at Cornerstone Church, I thought I might discover that the subject was taboo. The response was quite the opposite. I have watched women discover that forgiveness and cleansing really are available for every sin and mistake. The women of my church are so absolutely behind the ministry that I have enjoyed riding the wave of momentum with them as SaveOne has reached far beyond the walls of the local church to offer hope to an incredibly damaged part of our society.

I am so proud of Sheila for her passion, her vision, and her persistence as she has led the charge. The ministry of SaveOne has brought healing to the hurting. Now, she has captured this ministry in book form. You hold in your hand one of the greatest tools for one of the greatest problems of the Millennium. I encourage you to read it prayerfully and thoughtfully. You will not find condemnation here; you will find uncompromising truth that comes from a God who offers unlimited freedom.

—*Maury Davis*
Senior Pastor
Cornerstone Church

Introduction

I walked, but didn't know if my legs would carry me. I was terrified, not knowing what to expect. This was the last thing on earth I ever wanted or expected to do. I was only nineteen: How would I explain this to my parents? What if they were to say they were right about me all along? I thought I could just get this "problem" taken care of and not ever have to think about it again. I couldn't have been more wrong.

I signed in and was told I would receive counseling. My mind went wild thinking of how grateful I was that someone in charge was actually going to counsel me. I knew I needed to talk to someone who could give me an alternative; someone who didn't have all this craziness going on in her head like I did.

I was called into the office, where I was met by a cold and emotionless woman sitting behind a desk. I would later learn that a person validating wrongful death every day tends to be cold and aloof. I immediately burst into tears. I thought this would be my chance to describe what I was feeling, and that someone would help me. The woman simply asked, "Do you want to have this abortion?" I told her through my sobs, "I don't know any other choice." She wrote a number 2 on a small white card, handed it to me, and said, "Okay, then go sit in the waiting room and they'll call your number in a minute."

I was devastated. At that moment I realized that counseling was the last thing they were going to give me. I was nothing but 250 bucks to them. By the time my number was called, the room was filled to capacity, mostly with young girls just like me. They were lined around the walls, sitting on couches, chairs, and the floor. I stepped my way over and around them and went into an adjoining room. I lay down on the table and offered my first child to these strangers.

It was excruciatingly painful and an experience I will never forget. When I walked out of the abortion clinic that day, I was changed forever. How much I had changed was yet to be revealed.

The book you hold in your hands is what God gave me to help women find the emotional healing they need after an abortion. There is not a woman alive who grows up thinking that some day she is going to want to have an abortion. You could have been forced into thinking abortion was your only choice. You might have made the decision entirely on your own. Either way, if you have any form of regret, this book is for you.

I realize not all women suffer in the same way after an abortion. Some women, remarkably, have no lingering feelings of shame or regret, and for that I'm thankful. But others spend their entire lives trying to condone the choice they made, punishing themselves, being an emotional wreck, having nightmares, smothering their children to make up for the past, refusing to forgive themselves, having multiple abortions, etc.

This book was written to help you take this mantle from around your neck and lay it down. You've been carrying it around way too long. I'm here as an example of God's Grace and just how far it extends. After years of punishing myself with drugs, alcohol, a suicide attempt, and other things, I finally completed a study much like this one; a study that set me free after seven years of horrible emotional bondage.

This study can do the same for you. You may have had one abortion or more than you can remember. Either way, set your mind right now to complete this study. There might be days you think that this isn't worth the pain and memories you have to endure, but I encourage you to stick it out and look really hard for the light at the end of the tunnel. As you progress through each chapter, the light will grow brighter and more noticeable, until one day you wake up and find yourself standing in that light. I promise. I hope one day we will meet and you can tell me the story of when the Light showed Himself to you.

Introduction

While you're going through this book, I ask that you not jump ahead. There might be things in a later chapter that you would see and which you might think you could *never* do. Not to worry; all you have to do is work through one chapter at a time. Each week, focus on that one chapter and nothing else. This way, by the time you get to later chapters, you will be ready to handle those things.

Now that you're ready to get started, I want to say a prayer for you:

Heavenly Father,

I come to you today and ask your amazing grace to cover the woman holding this book. You know the grief she bears. You know the choices she has made. I ask that you walk with her, Father, through the next twelve weeks as she progresses through this study. You designed this book just for her; in fact, you had her in mind when you created this book. For that I'm thankful. Reveal your true self to her in a way in which she has never experienced. Let her know that her pain is not too much for you to bear. You have called us to lay our cares on you and you will give us rest. That's what she needs, Lord, rest from this burden she was never intended to bear. I thank you in advance for what you're going to do in this person's life. I've seen your miracles work in even the toughest cases. None are too big for you.

In Jesus's name I pray, Amen.

SaveOne

My Child,

Your struggle has been long. Your heartache has been heavy. You have cried and questioned and laid your heart on the altar of sorrows. I have been here with you through it all, as I will always be with you. But I am asking you today to make this choice: the choice to go on. For it is a choice in the end that only you can make—a choice to walk in the land of the living, to feel the sunshine and smile at the children, to be alive! A choice to believe that in spite of your loss and all it has cost you, there is much beauty and joy just outside your heart, waiting to be invited in. I have good plans for you, my child, if only you will choose to embrace them. They are plans rich with a new hope and a good future. There are people I love out there in that place called "the future." People who need what only you can give them—your smile, your wisdom, your comfort, your personality. Will you trust me to lead you to that good place? We will travel there together, one step at a time. I will be right beside you. Will you choose life?

Your loving Father, God.

Chapter One:
Your Source of Courage

Verse to memorize this week: *Give all your worries and cares to God, for He cares about what happens to you.* **1 Peter 5:7 NLT**

How do you picture God? As a little old man with a long white beard, sitting in a rocking chair? As a huge, scary, mean man standing up in heaven with bolts of lightning in each hand just waiting to zap you when you mess up? Or as your loving creator? Whatever your perception is, we will spend this chapter finding out if it is correct.

> *Disregard the study of God, and you sentence yourself to stumble and blunder through life blindfolded, as it were, with no sense of direction.*
>
> **J. I. Packer**

Describe how you picture God at this moment:

_____

_____

_____

Do you feel this is an accurate portrayal?

_____

Why or why not?

_____

_____

_____

_____

_____

Did you know that God is your protector, provider, hope, healer, father, and strength? He is able to see all that happens to you. He is able to calm any storm in your life. He is able to be there even when your friends and family aren't. He is able to give you a destiny. He is able to plan your future. He is able to open every door to get you to that future. He is able to put you back on the right path, even when you've chosen the wrong one. He is able to forgive you of your sins. He is able to send His very Son to die for you in order for that to happen. He is able to love you more than anyone on this earth has the capability to love. He is able to save your soul.

God's character does not change. Strain or shock can alter the character of a man, but nothing can alter the character of God.

J. I. Packer, Knowing God

This is the kind of God that created you. His name is Yahweh, the great I AM. When He appeared to Moses at the burning bush (**Exodus 3:1–14**), that is who He said He was. He is never changing. That is why He can describe Himself as I AM and we cannot. We are always changing: I am sad, I am hungry, I am happy. God isn't like that. His mood doesn't change with the season or at different times of the month. He said, "I AM," and that is who He is.

As you were reading the preceding text describing who God is and what He is able to do, did you have a connection with one of those scenarios?

_____

If so, which one?

_____

_____

Read **Genesis 16:13** and **Psalm 10:14**. Does it comfort you or unsettle you to think God sees all?

_____

_____

Why or why not?

_____

_____

_____

Read **Psalm 107:28–30**. Does it comfort you or unsettle you to think God can calm any storm in your life?

_____

Why?

_____

_____

_____

Read **Hebrews 13:5** and **Deuteronomy 31:6**. What do these verses tell you about God being there for you?

_____

_____

_____

Is there something you need that you feel God can't provide for you?

_____

_____

If so, what is that need?

_____

_____

_____

Read **Psalm 91**. What does that chapter mean to you?

_____

_____

_____

Now, read **Psalm 91**, again, out loud and in place of the word _you_ say the word _me, my,_ or _I_.

Can you see how God will protect you? The first verse states, _"You shall dwell in the secret place of the most high."_ It is saying you have an intimate place of divine protection, and no threat can ever overpower God. Verses **14–16** are God Himself speaking to you, telling you of the blessing He gives to those who know and love Him. Read this chapter often to remind you of God's protection.

～◎～

> _God never changes moods, cools off in His affections, or loses enthusiasm._
> **A. W. Tozer**

We are so limited in our human bodies—by life, age, weather patterns, wealth (or lack of it), social status, emotional baggage, our families, ideas that have been formed for us by our families, self-esteem, our government . . . the list goes on and on.

Do you realize God has no limits? He doesn't have an earthly body that ages and will eventually wear out. He isn't affected by weather patterns; He creates them. He doesn't care how much money you have or don't have; He is able to provide more or take away. He isn't impressed with your social status; He is the King of all Kings. He is saddened by the emotional baggage we carry; He wishes we would give it all to Him to carry. He hopes every day we will begin to see ourselves as He sees us, not as our family tells us we are.

Describe your relationship with God:

_____

_____

_____

Read **Psalm 139: 1–12.**
How do these verses explain the presence of God?

_____

_____

_____

Do you believe He is this active in your life?

_____

Why or why not?

_____

_____

God showed me He had been with me every day of my life, through every experience past and present. He showed me He even existed where no man or woman, including myself could ever go. He was in my tomorrows.
"Diane,"
in SaveOne
class

God is as close to you as you will allow Him to be. He created you for a purpose, with a destiny. There is a song written that says, "There's a God-shaped hole in all of us." I love that word picture. Many of us work to fill that hole with work, material things, friends, relationships, drugs, sex, and/or alcohol. I'm sure you could add your own "fillers" to that list. But the truth is, until you fill that hole with an intimate relationship with God, you will constantly be searching, never feeling truly satisfied. He wants you to come to Him with your burdens.

Read **Jeremiah 29:11** and write it below:

_____

_____

_____

Do you believe this promise is for you?

_____

_____

Write in your own words what this verse says to you:

_____

_____

_____

Read **Jeremiah 29:12** through the first sentence of **14**. There are three things He calls us to do in these verses. What are they?

_____

_____

_____

If we do these three things, what does He say He will do?

_____

_____

_____

> *Our God is a god who not merely restores, but takes up our mistakes and follies into His plan for us and brings good out of them. This is part of the wonder of his gracious sovereignty.*
>
> **J. I. Packer**

God's destiny for you never included abortion. When you chose to take a left fork onto the road called Abortion, you veered off into an area that wasn't part of His plan. He wants to steer you back onto the road He created for you. He wants to take this experience and turn it into something beautiful for Him. Only God can do that, and He will do it if you allow Him to.

Read **Genesis 50:20**. This verse tells you that what Satan means for evil in your life, God can turn to good. Do you believe God can do this in your life? Why or why not?

_____

_____

_____

_____

What do you feel your part in this procedure will be?

_____

_____

What steps can you take this week to get this process started?

_____

_____

_____

1 Samuel 16:7 says, *"For the Lord does not see as man sees; for man looks at the outward appearance, but the Lord looks at the heart."* God knows your heart. He knows your sorrow. He knows your regret. He knows your shame. He has seen how you have tried to deal with this on your own for so long. He has seen the ways you have worked to keep it secret. Now that you are dealing with the past, it's not a shock or a surprise to Him. He is happy that you have chosen at this time in your life to lay this burden down. These next few weeks are between you and only Him.

Write your memory verse in the space below:

_____

_____

_____

Take a moment and think about the time period between when you had your abortion and today. Can you think of some instances in which God was active in your life? Write them below and onto the next page:

_____

_____

_____

_____

_____

_____

_____

_____

_____

_____

_____

Do you believe God loves you?

_____

Why or why not?

_____

_____

_____

If you believe God doesn't love you, explain what you believe you would have to do in order to get God to love you again:

_____

_____

_____

Read **Romans 8:35–39.** What can separate the love of God from you?

_____

_____

_____

The New Living Translation says it best, I believe:

> *No, despite all these things, overwhelming victory is ours through Christ, who loved us. And I am convinced that nothing can ever separate us from His love. Death can't, and life can't. The angels can't, and the demons can't. Our fears for today, our worries about tomorrow, and even the powers of hell can't keep God's love away. Whether we are high above the sky or in the deepest ocean, nothing in all creation will ever be able to separate us from the love of God that is revealed in Christ Jesus our Lord.* **Romans 8:37–39 NLT**

All my days I have been aware of One going before me and with me, of doors ajar that I never could have opened.
Vance Havner

I believe that has to be one of the most beautiful scriptures in the entire Bible. Nowhere does it say, "But if you have an abortion, God will not take you back, or love you anymore." No, it says *nothing* can separate us from His love.

Now read **Psalm 30**. Write in your own words what you believe this Psalm means:

_____

_____

_____

Stop for a minute. Put down this book, close your eyes, and picture yourself with one of those heavy, wooden yokes around your neck. Imagine how your body has become carrying that yoke of abortion for as long as you've been carrying it. Now picture God reaching down and breaking it, crushing it to smithereens. There isn't even a piece left that you can hold in your fingertips. It's just dust lying at your feet. Give this yoke to God right now.

We have to allow God to destroy the yoke so it can never resume its previous position.

Read **Isaiah 10:27**. What does this verse say God will do for you?

_____

_____

_____

Throughout this chapter you have looked up many scriptures regarding who God is. This is by no means an exhaustive study, but should give you some idea of who God can be and wants to be in your life. Let's review. Look back at the beginning of this chapter and read your description of how you picture God.

Is that still an accurate portrayal?

_____

Does that portrayal line up with the scriptures you have read?

_____

Can you start to see God as who the Bible says He is?

_____

As you close this chapter, take a moment to pray and ask God to reveal Himself to you as the loving creator He really is. Write your prayer below:

_____

_____

_____

_____

_____

_____

_____

Your Source of Courage

Write your scripture memory verse for the week:

_____

_____

_____

> *Courage is the power to let go of the familiar.*
> **Pastor Maury Davis, Cornerstone Church**

What knowledge did you gain from working through this chapter?

_____

_____

_____

What steps can you take this week to put this knowledge into practice?

_____

_____

_____

Please use the blank pages that follow to write the thoughts you are having about this book. What are you feeling, thinking, and going through? This may not be comfortable for you, but just try it. There is something about writing your feelings out on paper that frees you. You will have room to write down your thoughts at the end of each chapter.

Journal Page

Journal Page

Journal Page

Journal Page

Journal Page

Chapter Two: What Happened to Me?

Verse to memorize this week: *Then Jesus said, 'Come to me all of you who are weary and carry heavy burdens, and I will give you rest.'* **Matthew 11:28 NLT**

The following comes from a journal written by Oswald Chambers. I include it here because I feel this writing is especially relevant for the women I talk to dealing with regret and shame from their abortion. Please read these words and see if they apply to your life.

"It is possible for people to become so accustomed to their bondage they resist efforts to free them. The Hebrews had been slaves in Egypt for four hundred years. Slavery meant they were not free to do God's will or go where they wanted. Moses had come to tell the Israelites how they could experience freedom, yet they were more concerned about the reaction of their taskmasters than they were about pleasing God. For them to be free would mean that the pharaoh they were serving would be angry! It would mean that the Egyptians they had served all their lives might attack them. Freedom from their slavery did not seem to be worth the hardships they would inevitably endure.

When God sets out to free us, there will often be a price we will have to pay. Grief can be a terrible form of bondage, yet we can become comfortable with it. We can grow so comfortable with fear that we don't know how to live without it. As destructive as our sinful habits and lifestyle might be, we may prefer living with the familiar, rather than being freed to experience the unknown. We may recognize the harmful influence of a friend but choose to reject God's will rather than offend our friend.

As incredible as it seems, the Israelites were angry with Moses for disrupting the life of slavery to which they had grown accustomed.

Have you been lulled into a comfortable relationship with your bondage? Do you fear change more than you fear God? Are you willing to allow God to do what is necessary in order to free you?"
—Oswald Chambers

> *Many of life's failures are people who did not realize how close they were to success when they gave up.*
> **Thomas Edison**

When the children of Israel left Egypt after years of slavery, they took forty years to complete an eleven-day journey. Why did that happen? They were stuck in a rut. God wanted to take them to a place of great abundance and victory, but they couldn't conceive God's plan. They had believed for so long that they would never see this place. In their minds, life didn't exist beyond their slavery. Instead of having faith in God to take them to this new place, they focused on their problems.

Read **Deuteronomy 1:6**.

God was telling them they had dwelled way too long at this one place. He was trying to motivate them to move forward, get on with their lives. The fact you are using this book is proof that you know God has brought you to this place to tell you the same thing. You have suffered long enough at this mountain in your life. It's time to allow Him to take you to a greater place of abundance. For this to happen, you must take the limits off God and raise your level of expectancy. That means you have to spend the next several weeks believing God is who He said He is, and He will do what He says He will do.

Read **Isaiah 61:7**.

The NLT says, *"Instead of shame and dishonor, you will inherit a double portion of prosperity and everlasting joy."* God will pay you back double, but He can't do this unless you go into this believing there is more for you. Don't accept this bondage from your abortion any longer. Don't live in mediocrity. Set a new standard for your life. Take the limits off God and allow Him to take the limits off your life. Step out in faith and believe God is about to do a great thing.

Throughout this chapter you will be answering questions and remembering details from your abortion experience. You may ask, "Why do I need to do this part?" The answer is, sometimes, when we go through a traumatic experience, we tend to exaggerate some details when remembering them. At other times we will forget details entirely because they are too painful to remember.

Whether your abortion experience was thirty years ago or one month ago, there are details that your mind has skewed as a protective device. In order to deal with this information properly you will need to bring these memories out of the shadows and into the light, where you can see them truthfully.

None of these questions are meant to judge you or make you feel bad, but only to help you remember. So please answer in as much detail as you can. Remember this, the answers to these questions are for your eyes only. Don't answer them according to how you think they should be answered, but answer the questions as truthfully as you can remember. This exercise is to help you recall the details, even though they may be painful. I encourage you to do this so you can deal with them and get on with your life.

> *Everything that is done in the world is done by hope.*
> Martin Luther

How old were you when you found out about your pregnancy?

_____

Where were you living? (city, state)

_____

With whom were you living?

_____

Were you married or single?

_____

Were you working at the time? If so, where?

_____

How many abortions have you had?

_____

(*If more than one, we suggest you go through this study concentrating on only one at a time. Please feel free to talk to your teacher more about this if you have any questions.*)

How did you feel when you found out about your pregnancy? Explain.

_____

_____

_____

Was God a part of your life during this time?

_____

Who was the father of your child?

_____

How old was he?

_____

How did you meet him?

_____

_____

Were you in love with him?

_____

Did you tell him about your pregnancy?

_____

If so, how did he react?

_____

_____

_____

How did his reaction affect you?

_____

_____

_____

Who else did you tell about your pregnancy?

_____

_____

What were their reactions?

_____

_____

How did their reactions make you feel?

_____

_____

_____

Who did you believe you couldn't tell about your pregnancy?
Why?

_____

_____

_____

_____

> *If you run into a wall, don't turn around and give up. Figure out how to climb it, go through it, or work around it.*
> **Michael Jordan**

Did you consider any alternatives to abortion? If so, what were they?

_____

_____

_____

_____

Why did you believe these alternatives weren't viable options?

_____

_____

_____

Was anyone else involved in the decision process? If so, who?

_____

_____

Did anyone encourage you to have an abortion? If so, who?
(List if more than one.)

_____

_____

_____

_____

What are your feelings toward this person (or persons) today?

_____

_____

_____

_____

What Happened to Me?

Did anyone encourage you to keep the child? If so, who?

_____

List if more than one.

_____

_____

_____

_____

What are your feelings toward this person (or persons) today?

_____

_____

> When you get into a tight place and everything goes against you, till it seems as though you could not hang on a minute longer, never give up then, for that is just the place and time that the tide will turn.
>
> **Harriet Beecher Stowe**

How much time went by between finding out about your pregnancy and having your abortion?

_____

How far along were you in your pregnancy at the time of abortion?

_____

Where did you go for your abortion?

_____

Who took you?

_____

Describe your feelings right before the abortion:

_____

_____

_____

Describe your feelings right after the abortion.

_____

_____

_____

Do you remember any of the people who worked at the facility? If so, who?

_____

_____

Is there anything that someone said to you while you were there that you've always remembered? If so, what?

_____

_____

_____

What type of abortion did you have?

_____

What details, if any, do you remember from the abortion procedure?

_____

_____

_____

What was your relationship with the father of your child like after the abortion?

_____

_____

_____

Do you have contact with him now?

_____

What lasting effects has the abortion left you with physically?

_____

_____

Mentally?

_____

_____

Emotionally?

_____

_____

Do you feel anger toward anyone from that period of your life? If so, explain:

_____

_____

_____

Do you feel bitterness toward anyone from that period of your life? If so, explain:

_____

_____

_____

_____

_____

Have you experienced any long periods of depression? If so, explain:

_____

_____

_____

What is your reaction when someone mentions the subject of abortion to you?

_____

_____

Are you able to talk about abortion without having a strong emotional reaction?

_____

Tears are the diamonds of heaven. **Charles Spurgeon**	How do you feel when you are around babies or small children? _____ _____

Think of all the responsibilities and activities in your life. Is there anything you are doing to try to pay for the guilt of your abortion? If so, what?

_____

_____

Have you in the past, or do you presently have nightmares that you believe stem from your abortion? If so, explain:

_____

_____

_____

What Happened to Me?

Have you done anything in the past, or are you currently doing anything, to punish yourself for your abortion? If so, explain:

_____

_____

_____

Did you begin to use drugs and alcohol, or did you increase the amounts, after your abortion? If so, explain:

_____

_____

_____

> *Pray harder when it's hardest to pray.*
> **Pastor Maury Davis, Cornerstone Church**

What was your perception of God at the time of your abortion?

_____

_____

_____

Did that perception change afterward? If so, explain:

_____

_____

_____

Have you ever tried or contemplated suicide? If so, explain:

_____

_____

_____

_____

_____

How could the knowledge you have gained about abortion be used to help others?

_____

_____

_____

What do you hope to gain by completing this book?

_____

_____

_____

After writing your answer to the last question, say it out loud. Now say a short prayer to God asking Him to help you gain what you want to gain by completing this book. Write your prayer below:

_____

_____

_____

_____

_____

What knowledge did you gain from working through this chapter?

_____

_____

_____

_____

_____

What steps can you take this week to put that knowledge into practice?

_____

_____

_____

_____

_____

Write your scripture memory verse for the week:

_____

_____

_____

Now that you have finished answering all these questions, perhaps you have remembered more than I have asked about. On the following pages, write any details you have remembered, then go back over the questions and add to your answers anything you deem necessary.

Journal Page

Journal Page

Journal Page

Journal Page

Chapter Three:
Dealing with Stray Emotions:
Part I

Verse to memorize this week: *Be anxious for nothing, but in everything by prayer and supplication, with thanksgiving, let your requests be made known to God; and the peace of God, which surpasses all understanding, will guard your hearts and minds through Christ Jesus.*
Philippians 4:6,7

hen a person experiences a trauma, such as abortion, there are different ways each individual deals with that trauma. Post Abortion Syndrome (PAS) is one of those ways. This syndrome affects millions of women (and men) all across our nation. The official definition is this:

> *By affliction, the Lord separates the sin that He hates from the soul that He loves.*
>
> **Rev. William Secker**

"The chronic inability to process the painful thoughts and emotions regarding a crisis pregnancy and subsequent abortion (guilt, anger, grief); identify the loss that was incurred, and come to peace with God, herself, and others." The symptoms associated with PAS is as follows:

- Feeling unresolved guilt regarding the abortion
- Having a heightened state of anxiety or apprehension
- Suppressing or denying that the abortion happened or was wrong
- Psychological numbing through suppressed feelings, substance abuse, etc.
- Depression
- Suicidal thoughts or tendencies
- Re-experiencing the abortion either through flashbacks or nightmares
- Preoccupation with becoming pregnant again
- Anxiety about childbearing issues, thinking God is going to punish you
- Interruption of bonding process with current children
- Remembering the anniversary of the abortion or the due date

If you connected with at least three of these symptoms, then you are probably suffering from PAS. Let me ask you a question: If you were to have a sickness that you couldn't shake after a month, would you go to your doctor? You would, wouldn't you? If you didn't, what do you think would happen to you? Your body? Your mind? Your job? Your relationships? Do you think they would suffer any? The wound from abortion is the same way. Abortion leaves a gaping hole in your life and your heart. It is a loss that is never grieved. My friend Donna explained it to me this way:

"Abortion is like a gunshot wound to the leg. If you were to be shot in the leg and you never told anyone, but just tried to deal with it on your own, what do you think would happen? You would go home, stop the bleeding, and put bandages on it as best you knew how. You would have to rethink your wardrobe, because you would only be able to wear pants to cover up the wound so no one could find out. Eventually, you would probably start to walk a little hunched over and with a limp because you had to deal with so much pain. The wound would eventually get infected and start to seep into your bloodstream and soon affect every limb of your body. The only way to get the wound healed at this point would be to take off all the layers of bandages, expose it to the light, scrape all the infection out, and let it breathe. This would take some time to totally heal, and would be extremely painful, but would be well worth it to get rid of the pain."

Did you see yourself in any of that explanation?

_____

Have you felt not right for a long time?

_____

Have you tried to deal with the pain from your abortion alone?

_____

Have you put layers of protection around yourself, so no one can get to you and find out about your abortion? If yes, how?

_____

_____

_____

Have you had to rethink the way you do things to keep this secret from everyone?

_____

Do you feel as if you are carrying a heavy burden?

_____

Has this burden affected other areas of your life? If so, how?

_____

_____

_____

Are you ready to expose your wound to the light so it can be healed?

_____

Now, let's break this down and be a little more specific. You have different emotions that are affected by the trauma of abortion. Let's deal with these different emotions individually.

The Emotion of Guilt

Everyone knows what guilt is. Everyone has experienced it. Guilt is when you know you've done something wrong and you beat yourself up afterward. That is my own definition. _Webster's_ says it is the fact of being responsible for the commission of an offense. So, fact is, you had an abortion. You are responsible for that choice.

It was very, very hard for me to believe, after all I had done, even after I abandoned God, He still, no matter how long it took me, forgave me.
"Monica," in SaveOne class

I know every situation is different. You might have been forced to go through with it, but unless the workers held you down on the table (which has happened) you were ultimately responsible.

Usually, there are three ways people deal with guilt. The first is by drowning it. Have you tried to drown your guilt with drugs, alcohol, eating, sex, or _____ ?

Write out your method of drowning your guilt:

_____

_____

_____

The second way people usually deal with guilt is by denying it. Our society has become more and more about manipulating or compromising our ethics to fit our situation. The lines for right and wrong have been blurred. We are now taught that guilt is an ancient concept, a rationalization that allows us to deny our choices are wrong. We find ourselves justifying our abortion instead of realizing it is sin, and a line we should not have crossed. How have you justified your abortion in the past?

_____

_____

_____

How have you denied that your choice was wrong?

_____

_____

_____

The third way people usually deal with guilt is by deflecting it. We blame other people for our bad choices. Maybe the abortion was not your choice, but like I said before, unless you were held down on the table, which has been known to happen, the choice was ultimately yours. It is time to accept responsibility, because until you do, you will never get to the root of guilt and know just how this choice has affected your life.

How long do you believe you should feel guilty? Three months? Three years? A lifetime?

_____

Name something from your past over which you felt guilt but don't anymore:

_____

What made the guilt go away?

_____

_____

_____

Are there things you are doing to remind yourself to feel guilty? If so, what are they?

_____

_____

_____

One thing I always did was put a star on my calendar on March 29 every year. That was the day I had my abortion. I felt as if I should kick myself for two weeks before and two weeks after. I would just be a wreck during that time. March 29 is now my youngest son's birthday. God truly wiped away my guilt.

There is no forgiveness from God unless you freely forgive your brother from your heart. And I wonder if we have been too narrow in thinking that "brother" only applies to someone else. What if YOU are the brother or sister who needs to be forgiven, and you need to forgive yourself? **David Seamands, Healing for Damaged Emotions**

Let's look to see what God tells us about guilt. Read **2 Samuel 11**. This is the story of David and the acts he committed. After reading this story, write below your thoughts toward David and what he did:

_____

_____

_____

Now read **Psalm 38:3–8**. David writes this passage after he has realized what he has done and how he grieved God. Does this describe the guilt you feel?

_____

Do you believe David should have felt guilty? If so, for how long?

_____

_____

Read **Acts 13:22**. God described David as "a man after my own heart, which shall fulfill all my will." God knew at this point the decisions, good and bad, that David would make.

Now let's read **Psalm 30**. How does this describe David now?

_____

_____

_____

Do you believe it is all right for David to feel this way after what he did? Why or why not?

_____

_____

_____

_____

Do you believe God can turn your mourning into dancing? Why or why not?

_____

_____

You can't drown, deny, or deflect the guilt of your abortion. You must dissolve it through Christ Jesus.

What did this section teach you about guilt?

_____

_____

_____

What steps can you take this week to allow God to start dissolving your guilt?

_____

_____

_____

❧

The Emotion of Anger

Anger is an odd emotion. It's OK that we get angry, but God instructs us not to sin while we're angry. (**Psalm 4:4**) I believe He tells us that for our own protection. We do crazy things in our anger that we regret later. When anger is allowed to fester, it turns to rage.

Explain one time in the past few weeks when you got angry:

_____

_____

_____

> *Anger is an acid that can do more harm to the vessel in which it is stored than to anything on which it is poured.*
> **The Baptist Beacon**

What was your response?

_____

_____

_____

Was it the correct response?

_____

If no, what could you have done differently?

_____

_____

_____

> "What is righteous indignation?" one child asked another. "I don't know, but I think it means to get real mad and not cuss."

Is your anger controlled? Or does your anger sometimes get out of control?

_____

Do you get angry over stupid things? If so, give an example.

_____

_____

_____

After an abortion, some women will have angry outbursts and not understand where those outbursts come from. This comes from having anger that has been forced underneath the surface. It starts boiling underneath that surface, and at one little opening it all comes gushing out like an erupting volcano. One way my anger was out of control was when I would be driving. It was like everyone around me had to watch out for me. If they didn't, that was it. I would yell and scream and keep my thumb on the horn at all times just waiting to tell someone what I thought of him or her. I have been known to swerve at people to scare them after they cut me off or were going too slow for my taste. I know you're thinking I must have been a tyrant. Actually, I was. When I see someone acting like that now, I just laugh and let that person go in front of me, or I wave to them and smile.

What area of your life has a lot of anger in it?

_____

What good does this anger do you?

_____

_____

Read **Proverbs 25:28**. What does this verse tell you about controlling your anger?

_____

_____

_____

Read **Proverbs 15:1** and **Proverbs 16:32**.
What do these two verses tell you about anger?

_____

_____

_____

To accomplish being slow to anger, and to acquire the ability to speak soft words, what trait would you have to master?

_____

_____

_____

Do you believe you can master self-control on your own? Why or why not?

_____

_____

_____

> *I used to count to ten when becoming angry. But one day I thought of the first ten words of the Lord's Prayer. Now instead of counting to ten, I slowly say, 'Our Father which are in Heaven, hallowed be thy name.'*
>
> **Mrs. Fulton Oursler, whose husband wrote the classic book, *The Greatest Story Ever Told***

If self-control doesn't come easy for you when it comes to anger, God is there to help you refine that quality. You don't have to master it on your own. In fact, it's much easier when you allow God to work through you.

~⊙~

What did this section teach you about anger?

_____

_____

_____

What steps can you take this week to begin allowing God to work through you in the area of anger?

_____

_____

_____

_____

Following are some more verses to study regarding anger. After reading these verses, turn to the journal pages at the end of this chapter and write your feelings about anger and what you have learned in this section about anger:

Dealing with Stray Emotions: Part I

Psalm 37:8

Proverbs 14:17

Proverbs 17:27

Proverbs 19:19

Hebrews 12:15

Ephesians 4:26

The Emotion of Sorrow

Sorrow: Mental suffering or pain caused by injury, loss, or despair. That's the definition *Webster's* gives us. Is this the way you feel when you think about your abortion? You're not alone. Abortion is a loss. Many people don't understand that, even though they chose to have an abortion, it is still a loss they were never allowed to grieve. Grieving is a process you have to endure when you experience a loss. When you don't go through the grieving process, you stop growing in that area of your life, and you learn to just "manage" this unresolved grief. Until you allow yourself to grieve the loss of your child, you will always just be "managing" this sorrow instead of working through it and getting rid of it.

Draw a picture of a person full of sorrow:

Read **Psalm 6:6**.
Is this how you feel inside?

_____

Have you learned to manage your sorrow so well you believe there is none?

_____

Read **Psalm 34:18**. Take a moment, put down this book, and talk to God. Concentrate solely on Him. Turn off any television, radio, or anything else that might distract you. Get alone and talk to God. Ask Him to reveal to you your hidden sorrow and which areas of your life have been affected. When you ask, He will answer. Don't discount what He tells you. Take as much time as you need.

What areas of your life have been affected by sorrow?

_____

_____

_____

> *Who doesn't make mistakes?! But the greatest error of all is to let any mistake destroy your faith in yourself. The only sensible course is to study and analyze why you made the mistake. Learn all you can from it, then forget it and go ahead. Figure on doing better next time.*
> **Norman Vincent Peale**

Read **John 11:1–44**. The people who were present after Lazarus died were full of sorrow. They had experienced the loss of Lazarus. They had no hope. With their human eyes, they saw Lazarus was dead and believed that was the end. But was it? When Jesus gets involved, things change. When you look at your situation with human eyes you have no hope. You can't turn back the clock and make a different choice. You can't bring your child back and make everything all right. But is that the end of the story? No. Jesus can turn your sorrow into gladness and your mourning into dancing. I don't know how, but I know He can; I've experienced it firsthand. I lived for seven years with the horrific memory of abortion. When I allowed Jesus to work in my life, and I allowed myself to receive His working, things changed.

46

The only way I can describe it is to say it was a supernatural transformation. I went from hating myself to loving Christ. I went from contemplating suicide on a regular basis, to enjoying life again. I went from thinking of my dead child, to picturing her in heaven alive and well. I went from my secret shame, to telling others so they could experience the same transformation. This didn't happen to me because I'm more special than others. This happened because Jesus loves me in a way that no one else ever can. He loves you that same way. He wanted to wipe away my sorrow and tears. Just like Jesus, who in a moment's notice raised Lazarus from the dead, He wiped away their sorrow. He can wipe away yours, too.

Spend the next few moments talking to Jesus. Pour out your sorrow; tell Him how it has affected you. Tell Him you're ready to receive all He has for you. Be honest with Him and allow Him to work in your life. Then be very still and listen. He's there.

> *When I first started the class I had no intention of "unveiling" my true self, or emotions. Somehow, without me even being aware of it, my shell was cracked and eventually removed.*
> **"Julie," in SaveOne class**

Read **Isaiah 51:3**. The comfort He is giving to Zion is the same promise He is telling you today.

Write your scripture memory verse for the week:

_____

_____

_____

What did this section teach you about sorrow?

_____

_____

_____

_____

_____

What steps can you take this week to allow God to rid you of your sorrow?

_____

_____

_____

_____

_____

_____

Journal Page

Journal Page

Journal Page

Journal Page

Chapter Four:
Dealing with Stray Emotions:
Part II

Verse to memorize this week: *Fear not; you will no longer live in shame. The shame of your youth and the sorrows of widowhood will be remembered no more.* **Isaiah 54:4 NLT**

A lot of people confuse guilt and shame, thinking they are the same emotion. They're not. Guilt says, "I made a mistake." Shame says, "I am a mistake." Shame goes to the core of your personhood. It is an internal feeling of you. This comes from your perception of who you think you should be, compared to who you believe you really are. The bigger the difference, the deeper the shame. ALL of this comes from your belief system: who you believe you are; the thoughts you believe about yourself; what you believe others are thinking of you. It's that belief system that has to be changed. Look up **Romans 12:2**. Write this verse below:

> *You can't take your failures and let them determine who you are. Identity isn't based on failure, but on Jesus Christ.*
> **Pastor Maury Davis, Cornerstone Church**

_____

_____

_____

_____

Renewing your mind is a simple thing, but it's a lifelong journey. Part of renewing your mind is realizing where these wrongful thoughts come from. Lewis Smedes put it best when he said, "All unhealthy shame is rooted in deceit." Sure, you made a wrong choice when you had an abortion. But what you have to realize is that living in shame for the

Shame: painful feelings when there is a difference between who I think I should be and who I really am.

Taken from Hope Clinic training manual

rest of your life isn't going to make it right, nor is it going to improve your life in any way. My pastor, Maury Davis, said it best in one of his sermons, "When you live your life in shame, you are living beneath your destiny, destroying your sense of value. You *have* to renew your mind, and then you begin to think differently about your problems." Renewing your mind doesn't happen overnight. It comes from a consistent study and meditation on God's Word. Getting this word into your mind will release the bondage of shame from your life, tearing the root of deceit out of you that Satan has had there way too long.

What are some of the things Satan has made you believe about yourself?

_____

_____

_____

Do the following shame statements sound familiar in any way?

"If you knew me, you wouldn't love me."

"I'm worthless."

"There's no hope for me."

"I've made too many mistakes."

"I don't deserve to be forgiven."

Add your own to the list. Write down three of your own shame statements:

1. _____

2. _____

3. _____

Dealing with Stray Emotions: Part II

Look up **Mark 10:27.** What does this verse mean to you?

_____

_____

_____

Do you believe it is possible for God to change your thought process?

_____

How will God achieve this?

_____

_____

_____

Look up **II Corinthians 10:4–5.** What is your part in this process?

_____

_____

_____

How will you bring thoughts captive to the obedience of Christ?

_____

_____

_____

> All unhealthy
> shame is
> rooted in
> deceit.
> **Lewis Smedes**

When you close a door to Satan, he eventually leaves you alone in that area because you are not vulnerable there anymore.

While you are going through this study, you will get in the habit of looking up scriptures, memorizing scriptures, and studying God's Word. I challenge you to not let this be the end of your study. The Bible holds the answers to all of life's questions. It is as relevant in today's world as it was thousands of years ago when it was written. There are many, many studies available, just like this one, that go into other areas of your life. One that I've done is called *The Mind of Christ*, by Hunt and King. Another is *Experiencing God*, by Blackaby and King. A must-have is *The Battlefield of the Mind*, by Joyce Meyer. Just pick one after you're through with this one and do it. Then pick another and do it. You're not in a hurry; you just want to remain consistent. If you continue, one day you will run across this book and remember this time. You will flip open the pages and read your answers and be shocked that you ever felt the way you do. You will see in vivid detail what God truly can do when you open yourself to Him and allow Him to change your thought process by renewing your mind. We will study more about renewing your mind in chapter eight.

What did this section teach you about shame?

_____

_____

_____

What steps can you take this week to start thinking differently about yourself?

_____

_____

_____

Dealing with Stray Emotions: Part II

The Emotion of Depression

Read **Psalm 6:2**. If you battle with depression, is this how you feel sometimes?

_____

Now read **Psalm 34:18**. Where is God when you are depressed?

_____

> Living beneath your destiny destroys your sense of value.
> **Pastor Maury Davis, Cornerstone Church**

Look up **Proverbs 17:22**. Satan wants more than anything else to keep your spirit broken through depression. This verse says it "dries up your bones." You could reword that to say it dries up your entire life.

Describe your depression below. Be specific. What do you do when you're depressed? Do you stay in the house with the blinds closed? Do you drink alcohol? Do you stay in the bed and remain inactive? Do you overeat? Do you become irritable and crabby? Do you want to stay away from people?

_____

_____

_____

Is this response a cure for depression or an intensifier for depression?

_____

Draw your idea of what a depressed face looks like:

57

SaveOne

List below at least ten activities that are cures for depression:

1. _____

2. _____

3. _____

4. _____

5. _____

6. _____

7. _____

8. _____

9. _____

10. _____

Dealing with Stray Emotions: Part II

Read **Psalm 61:1–2**.
This is a metaphor to remind us that it doesn't matter where we are, there is always a higher place to go as long as we trust and rely on God. When your heart is overwhelmed, cry out to God and ask Him to lead you to the higher rock.

Read **Lamentations 3:22–23**.
Does God ever run out of mercy or compassion for you?

_____

_____

Read **Isaiah 40:31** and write it below:

_____

_____

_____

_____

> *Long-term depression over my abortion robs me of the ability to live a healthy, productive life. Depression consumes all of my energy. I can learn not to surrender to crippling depression.*
> **Taken from A Season to Heal, by Luci Freed and Penny Salazar**

What does this verse say He will do for you when you are depressed and lean on, trust in, and wait on God?

_____

_____

_____

After reading all this scripture on depression, do you believe you will ever feel as though you are alone when you get depressed?

_____

Read **Psalm 46:1** and **Isaiah 40:29**. What is God telling you in both of these scriptures?

_____

_____

_____

What did this section teach you about depression?

_____

_____

_____

What steps will you take this week to cure your depression?

_____

_____

_____

Write your memory verse for the week:

_____

_____

_____

❧

The Emotion of . . .

Write the name of any stray emotion that was not covered that you believe stems from your abortion:

_____

_____

Read **Psalm 34:19.** Do you believe God can deliver you? Why or why not?

_____

_____

_____

_____

Dealing with Stray Emotions: Part II

Look up at least three scriptures that pertain to this emotion, either through your Bible's concordance or a Bible website search. Write the scripture references below:

_____

_____

_____

Is there at least one of these verses that you can relate to? If so, which one?

_____

Write it below:

_____

_____

_____

Smooth seas do not make skillful sailors.
African proverb

Why do you relate to this one?

_____

_____

_____

Is there at least one verse that advises how to deal with this emotion? If so, which one?

_____

How?

_____

_____

What did this section teach you about this emotion?

_____

_____

_____

_____

> *Connected with Him in His love, I am more than a conqueror; without Him, I am nothing.*
>
> **Corrie Ten Boom**

What steps can you take this week to get this emotion under control?

_____

_____

_____

_____

Using what you have learned so far in this book, take the next few pages and write about this stray emotion. Take your time and write out your feelings, your struggles, and the cures for not letting this emotion get the best of you. Then write out anything else you have learned about your emotions through this chapter.

Journal Page

Journal Page

Journal Page

Chapter Five:
Forgiving Others

Verse to memorize this week: *And whenever you stand praying, if you have anything against anyone, forgive him, that your Father in heaven may also forgive you your trespasses.* **Mark 11:25-26**

or many of you, just reading the name of this chapter makes your heart rate go up. You have someone in your life that was actively involved in your abortion experience who you know you need to forgive. Others of you won't be able to think of anyone you haven't been able to forgive. If you are one of those, don't assume you can skip this chapter. This part is just as relevant to you as it is to the woman whose heart is racing right now. A lack of forgiveness that stays on the backburner has the ability to poison your life if you let it.

> *The sin of unforgiveness is a cancer that destroys relationships, eats away at one's own psyche, and, worst of all, shuts us off from God's grace.*
>
> Robertson McQuilkin

We're going to go back and figure out exactly whom you may harbor any ill will toward, and we will get that resolved in this chapter. Forgiving someone doesn't always happen overnight, but we will start the journey together.

Look back in Chapter 1 at the question that asked about your feelings toward any person who encouraged you to have an abortion. Also, look at the question that asked you to write down anyone toward whom you still felt anger or bitterness. What were your answers to these questions?

_____

_____

_____

_____

When you think of these people, do you experience any type of negative reaction? If so, what?

_____

_____

_____

Let's look at an example of forgiveness. Read the following:

Genesis 37:3–4.
Genesis 37:23–28.
Genesis 39.
Genesis 41:14–15.
Genesis 41:37–41.
Genesis 42:6–8.
Genesis 45:1–15.

> *Doing an injury puts you below your enemy; revenging one makes you even with him; forgiving it sets you above him.*
>
> **Anonymous**

Can you believe all that Joseph endured? His brothers hated him, and he hadn't even done anything wrong. They were just jealous. He was thrown into a pit and left for dead, then sold into slavery by his brothers. When he got to Egypt, he had to work as a slave. He was then framed for attempted rape and thrown into prison. Even through all of this, he never stopped trusting God. That was the one constant in Joseph's life; trust in God. Because of this trust, God was with him and he flourished everywhere he went. He was able to interpret Pharaoh's dream. Because of that he was made the number-two man in all of Egypt. God took a horrible situation and turned it to Joseph's good because of his constant trust in God. Isn't it ironic that the brothers who hated Joseph so much had to turn to him in their time of need? Can you see how God worked in Joseph's life? Explain:

_____

_____

_____

_____

How did Joseph react to his brothers when they showed up for help?

_____

_____

_____

I admire Joseph for being able to still love and forgive his brothers. He had to endure all he did because of his brothers, but yet he didn't hold a grudge against them. It would have been very easy for Joseph to withhold what his brothers needed out of spite. If he had done that instead, do you think God would have remained such a constant in Joseph's life?

_____

Read **Luke 6:37** and write it below:

_____

_____

_____

I know forgiving others is a very hard thing to do. It is especially hard to forgive if the other person shows no remorse. Look back at your verse to memorize this week. What does it say about the other person's not being sorry for what they did? It doesn't say anything about the conditions you put on your forgiveness. The scripture simply says to forgive others, so you can be forgiven.

Read **2 Thessalonians 1:6–7**. In verse **6**, what does it state God will do for you?

_____

_____

_____

_____

Read **Romans 12:17–21.**
What does Christ tell us to do to our enemies?

_____

_____

_____

Read **Matthew 26:57–66.**
Why do you think Jesus didn't take up for Himself?

_____

_____

_____

Read **1 Peter 2:21–23.**
Jesus had perfect confidence in His Father, knowing He would judge his enemies justly.

⟡

Let's look at another example of forgiveness.
Read **Acts 7:59–60.**
What was happening to Stephen?

_____

_____

_____

_____

Does it say the people who were stoning him were sorry?

_____

_____

How did Stephen react?

_____

_____

Which people associated with your abortion experience have you thought about forgiving if they showed remorse?

_____

_____

_____

_____

_____

Who are you hurting by holding this grudge?

_____

Let's take a look at you for a moment. Write below a time when you did something wrong to someone and they forgave you for it:

_____

_____

How did it make you feel?

_____

_____

Did it change the way you thought of that person? If so, how?

_____

_____

_____

_____

Why do you think God stresses so much in the Bible that we are to forgive others?

_____

_____

_____

Read **Luke 23:34**.
Jesus forgave these men even though He knew they were about to kill Him. This is the ultimate example of forgiveness for us. Jesus paved the way for us to follow.

Read **Matthew 5:43–46**.
What are the four things that verse 44 instructs us to do?

> A Christian will find it cheaper to forgive than to resent. Forgiveness saves the expense of anger, the cost of hatred, the waste of spirits.
> **Hannah More**

_____

_____

_____

_____

_____

Does it say anywhere in that passage to seek revenge on the people who have hurt you?

_____

Write **Matthew 5:43–44**:

_____

_____

_____

_____

_____

_____

These scriptures go totally against our human nature. But God put them in the Bible for a reason. John Bevere (an exceptional author and speaker—I suggest reading any of his books) said it best when, in talking about these very verses, he said, "When we do this our hearts are healed and cannot become critical or jaded."

Make a list of every person involved in your abortion experience to whom you still harbor ill feelings. Think back to the decision-making and all the way up through to the present day. Write the names of everyone. It could be the father, the doctor who performed the abortion, society for making abortion legal, or a family member for throwing the abortion in your face. Take your time and write this list below. If you run out of lines, keep writing somewhere until you get every name down on paper:

_____

_____

_____

_____

_____

Now take each of these names and say a prayer to God. Individually, ask God to help you forgive them. Be specific; ask Him to take your thoughts captive when you think of each person in a negative way. Ask Him to help you love them and soften your heart toward them. Then pray for something positive to happen in their life. Take this prayer very seriously, because it can change your life if you believe what you are praying can and will happen.

It's the only solution I have found to retaliation and revenge, the only way I've been able to get past blame and resentment, the only antidote for secret, smoldering feelings of rage from the pain of my past. Forgiveness. Not until I fully forgave my offenders, one by one, name-by-name, offense-by-offense, did I gain the mastery over those tendencies within me to get back or to get even. I'm suggesting you will discover the same is true for you.

Charles Swindoll, Esther

Now, let's pray again. Put down this book and say a heartfelt prayer to God. Ask His forgiveness for holding this grudge toward these people for so long.

Now that you have asked forgiveness for all these things, that doesn't mean you won't have feelings and thoughts come up again toward these people. If and when that happens, don't tell yourself you failed or that it didn't really work. Instead, remember this time and your prayer. God heard you and will bring your prayer to fruition if you continue to guard your heart and keep bad thoughts of these people away.

Write **Philippians 4:6–8**:

_____

_____

_____

_____

_____

_____

_____

_____

What do these verses tell us to think about?

_____

_____

_____

_____

These verses are in the Bible because God knew we would have bad thoughts come into our minds. He is instructing us here on what to think about, so we can keep the ill will and the bitterness from creeping back into our lives.

I remember reading a certain story about forgiveness. It's about a man named Rev. Walter H. Everett. He answered the phone one night only to hear the words no parent is ever ready to hear: "Scott was murdered last night." Walter's anger toward his son's killer raged, growing even worse when a plea bargain resulted in a reduced sentence for the attacker.

His rage affected his entire life. He wondered how he would ever let go of the anger and forgive. "The answer came the first time I saw Mike, almost a year after Scott's death. Mike stood in court prior to his sentencing and said he was truly sorry for what he had done. Three-and-a-half weeks later, on the first anniversary of Scott's death, I wrote to Mike. I told him about my anger and asked some pointed questions. Then I wrote, 'Having said all that, I want to thank you for what you said in court, and as hard as these words are for me to write, I forgive you.' I wrote of God's love in Christ and invited Mike to write to me if he wished.

> *Real forgiveness means looking steadily at the sin, the sin that is left over without any excuse, after all allowances have been made, and seeing it in all its horror, dirt, meanness, and malice, and nevertheless being wholly reconciled to the man who has done it.*
> **C. S. Lewis**

"Three weeks later his letter arrived. He said that when he read my letter, he couldn't believe it. No one had ever said to him, 'I forgive you.' That night he had knelt beside his bunk and prayed for, and received, the forgiveness of Jesus Christ. Additional correspondence led to regular visits during which we spoke often of Mike's (and my) growing relationship with Christ. Later I spoke on Mike's behalf before a parole board, and he was given an early release. In November 1994, I was the officiating minister at his wedding.

"When asked about his early release, Mike says, 'It felt good, but I was already out of prison. God had set me free when I asked for his forgiveness.'"

Can I truly forgive? I had wondered if it were possible. But I've discovered the meaning of the Apostle Paul's words: "For freedom Christ has set us free."

∽◐∾

What did this section teach you about forgiving others?

_____

_____

_____

What steps can you take this week to further heal these relationships?

_____

_____

_____

Write your memory verse for the week:

_____

_____

_____

Use one of the journal pages that follow to write what you would like to say to the people you have forgiven through this chapter.

> *I conquer only where I yield.*
> **Sister Alice Jane Blythe**

∽◐∾

Journal Page

Journal Page

Journal Page

Chapter Six: God's Grace

Verse to memorize this week: *Let us therefore come boldly to the throne of grace, that we may obtain mercy and find grace to help in time of need.* **Hebrews 4:16**

$\mathcal{W}$hat is your definition of grace?

_____

_____

For years I didn't really have a definition of grace. Grace was one of those churchy words I grew up hearing all the time and singing about, but I never took the time to really think about what grace meant. One day I was asked to give a talk at a spiritual retreat. The topic was grace. As I studied for my talk, the understanding of God's grace really became clear to me. Grace means "undeserved love and favor." Write that in the space provided:

_____

How many times in our lives have we withheld something from someone, or something was withheld from us because we didn't "deserve" it? God doesn't think that way. He created us, and He has an unending supply of undeserved love and favor with your name on it.

Write your name in the blank:

_____ has an unending supply of love and favor.

SaveOne

Read **I Peter 2:9** and write it below:

_____

_____

_____

_____

Who does this verse say you are?

_____

_____

Let's look at some examples of God's grace and how far it extends. Remember back in chapter five, where we read a little bit about Stephen and how he forgave the people who were stoning him?

Read **Acts 7:58**.
This mentions a man named Saul. Pay attention to him. Let's read a little bit more about who he was and what he was about.

Read **Acts 8:1, 3**.
Saul had a murderous hatred for all Christians. He gave the go-ahead to kill Stephen because Stephen was a Christian. Saul also led the persecution against the church as written in verse one. Saul murdered and imprisoned innocent people simply because they believed in God.

Read **Acts 9:1–9**.
This chapter starts out telling us about Saul's receiving even more authority to imprison Christians. He is on his journey, when the audible voice of Jesus Christ speaks to him. I believe that got his attention, because he fell to the ground. Jesus asks Saul why he is persecuting Him. He asked this because attacking a child of God is a direct attack on Christ Himself. He then struck Saul blind for three days. My opinion is that He had to do that to get Saul to slow down long enough to think about what was going on. Sometimes we get too busy with our lives. There are moments when we don't take the time to just simply sit and listen to what God has to tell us, even when we

are working for Christ. This was a huge turning point in Saul's life. God wanted him to realize the seriousness of what was about to happen.

Read **Acts 9:20–22**.
Saul did a complete turnaround, didn't he? He immediately started telling people that Jesus was Lord. God extended His grace to Saul, who had committed murder, victimized the church, and imprisoned innocent believers.

Remember the definition of grace? What is it?

_____

_____

Saul definitely received undeserved love and favor. What does this story tell you about God's Grace?

_____

_____

John Bevere has another definition for grace: "God's empowering presence." Saul experienced God's presence. It is that presence in our lives that empowers us to do things we normally could not. Because of God's Grace, Saul was truly forgiven and changed. He became one of the greatest witnesses for Christ in history.

Read **2 Corinthians 9:8**.
Do you believe this same Grace is for you today? Why or why not?

_____

_____

_____

_____

_____

Read **Joel 2:25**, and write it below:

_____

_____

_____

Read **Ephesians 2:8–9**.
Saved doesn't just mean salvation. It can mean anything Satan may throw at you; bondage, guilt, shame, regret, sin in anger, depression. Our works cannot save us from these things, but laying these things down allows Jesus Christ to save us from it by His grace; His undeserved love and favor.

Read **Isaiah 55:7**.
What are the three actions we have to take?

1. _____

2. _____

3. _____

After these three actions, what does that verse say God will then do?

_____

_____

_____

Have you ever asked God to forgive you for your abortion?

_____

_____

Read **Matthew 7:7–11**. What do these verses tell you about asking something of God? Write your answer on the next page:

God's Grace

_____

_____

_____

∽❧∼

If you have never asked God to forgive you for the sin of abortion, I would like for you to take a moment, put down this book, and talk to God as you would a friend. Confess your abortion to Him (**Psalm 32:5**), talk to Him about it, and ask Him to forgive you. Take as long as you need. This is between you and God. After doing this, write below how this exercise made you feel and what you gained from it:

_____

_____

_____

_____

_____

_____

_____

_____

_____

_____

_____

_____

Read **Isaiah 38:17** and **Psalm 103:12**. What does God do with our sin once we have asked forgiveness?

_____

_____

_____

To be free from the power of sin, to be made to love holiness, is true happiness. A man who is holy is at peace with the creation, and he is in harmony with God. It is impossible for that man to suffer for long. He may for a while endure suffering for his lasting good; but as certainly as God is happy, the person who is holy must be happy.
Charles Spurgeon, God's Grace to You

Did you know God cannot tell a lie? He is perfect and without sin. If His word states He will remove our sin from us as far as the east is from the west, then that is what He HAS to do.

Write **Isaiah 43:25**:

_____

_____

_____

_____

Through what you have learned in this chapter, write in your own words how God forgives you of your sin:

_____

_____

_____

_____

_____

You may not instantly "feel" forgiven. Don't worry about that. Don't even think about it. What you have to know for sure is that your forgiveness is not based on your feelings. Think of how your feelings change from day to day. One day you might feel happy, the next day you might feel beautiful, and yet the next day you might feel irritable. That doesn't change who you truly are just because you feel differently from day to day. So one could only suppose the same is true with your feelings of forgiveness. Believe the scriptures you have studied over the past weeks. Know that you know that you have been forgiven.

What did this section teach you about God's Grace?

_____

_____

_____

What steps can you take this week to put this knowledge into practice?

_____

_____

_____

Write your memory verse for the week:

_____

_____

_____

Close this chapter by reading **Psalm 32**. In fact, read it three times. Get it in your mind and remember it always, so on those days you don't "feel" forgiven, you can turn to this chapter and remember God's Grace.

Journal Page

Journal Page

Journal Page

Journal Page

Chapter Seven: Can I Forgive Myself?

Verse to memorize this week: *For you shall know the truth, and the truth shall make you free. For if the Son makes you free, you shall be free indeed.* **John 8:32, 36 NLT**

*W*e've talked a lot about forgiveness throughout this book, but what we're about to discuss in this chapter is all about you. For now don't think about anyone you wrote about in the previous chapters. I only want you to think about yourself all during this week.

David Seamands, author of *Healing for Damaged Emotions*, writes "There is no forgiveness from God unless you freely forgive your brother from your heart. And I wonder if we have been too narrow in thinking that "brother" only applies to someone else. What if *you* are the brother or sister who needs to be forgiven, and you need to forgive yourself?"

Let's review your progress. So far you have developed a proper perspective of the loving, forgiving God He wants to be in your life. He is your source of courage! Through your asking, God has crushed that heavy wooden yoke of abortion you had been carrying around your neck for way too long. You made yourself remember details of your abortion experience so as to bring those memories out of the darkness and into the light. You realized that is the only way to heal this wound. You finally were able to put a name—Post Abortion Syndrome—to your symptoms. You have dealt with your emotions of guilt, shame, sorrow, depression, and anger. You have learned of true forgiveness and pinpointed the people involved in your abortion experience you needed to forgive. Then as hard as it was, you forgave them. You have learned about God's grace—undeserved love and favor, and just how far it extends. You have asked God to forgive you

> *It doesn't matter where you were burned; it matters where you are built.*
> **Pastor Maury Davis, Cornerstone Church**

for your abortion, and through this same grace He has. Be proud of yourself for making such progress! Did you realize all of what you had accomplished over the past few weeks?

Now we only have a little way to go before this time of healing will be complete. Like I said at the beginning of the chapter, this week we're going to focus on you.
Write **Romans 8:37**:

In the Macarthur Study Bible, the explanation for this verse states this: to conquer completely without any real threat to personal life or health.

Are you ready to conquer this thing once and for all?

Read **Romans 3:23**.
Who does this verse say has sinned?

My pastor (Maury Davis) told me one time, "Your righteousness lives in your faith, not your feelings, not your circumstances. If you abide in Christ, you are always on steady ground." We have to remember to have faith in knowing we are forgiven and not go by our feelings or our circumstances. Those things change constantly, but who Christ is and what He has done in our life does not change.

Can I Forgive Myself?

Read **Philippians 4:6–7**.

What do these verses tell you your actions have to be?

_____

_____

_____

What do these verses tell us Christ will do?

_____

_____

_____

I've written out of the New Living Translation, **Mark 11:24**. I like this version because it's plain and to the point: "Listen to me! You can pray for anything, and if you believe, you will have it."

❧

Like I stated in a previous chapter, God cannot tell a lie. If it is written in the Bible, it is the absolute truth. God will not waver from that. If you are truly sick of carrying this burden around, then it's time to pray. I don't want you to start thinking you are not worthy to pray this prayer. *None* of us are worthy regardless of what our past holds; that's when God's Grace and our faith are enacted. Pray this prayer with boldness and authority from God. He has brought you this far, He's not about to leave you now. Let go of the bad thoughts you are having about yourself and prepare your mind to pray.

> *Change is both a challenge and a threat. It represents everything I hope for, and everything I fear.*
> **Dale Hansenbourke**

In a passage in **Luke** (**11:1**), one of Jesus's disciples asked Him to teach them how to pray. Jesus replied, "When you pray, say Our Father which art in heaven, Hallowed be thy name. Thy kingdom come. Thy will be done in earth, as [it is] in heaven. Give us this day our daily bread. And forgive us our debts, as we forgive our debtors. And lead us not into temptation, but deliver us from evil. For thine is the kingdom, and the power, and the glory, forever. Amen."

Now, I realize that that is a prayer you've heard before. You may have breezed through it because it was so familiar, but let's study it for a moment. You start out talking to your Father, and you tell Him that hallowed is His name. Hallowed is praise. You're telling God His name you want to set apart as being holy, respected, and honored. You're telling God you want His kingdom to come soon. You want His will to be done here where you are, just as it would be if you were in heaven. You are asking God for your daily bread, which could be translated to mean your entire daily needs. He is teaching us right here to trust Him daily, and let tomorrow worry about itself. Then you asked His forgiveness for your sins (debts) because you are forgiving those who have sinned against you. As you learned in previous chapters, these two go hand in hand. Then you have asked Him to not let you be led in to temptation or to do things you know you shouldn't, but to take you away (deliver) you from any evil. Evil isn't just the big ones, sex outside marriage, drugs, alcohol, etc. Evil can be wrong thoughts, unforgiveness, the list goes on. Anything that doesn't line up with scripture can be considered evil if used in the wrong way. Then the prayer is again closed with praise.

One of the dear saints of God I have the privilege of knowing is Sister Alice Jane Blythe. She asked me to eat lunch with her one day. I was very honored. While at lunch, she told me of a family situation she was in one time, and how she allowed Satan to make her worry. She tossed and turned for nights, and she had a hard time concentrating on anything. Finally, God woke her up one night and told her to pray. He said, "Pray this way, Our Father which art in heaven, hallowed be thy name, thy kingdom come, thy will be done on earth as it is in heaven. Give us this day our daily bread. And forgive us our debts, as we forgive our debtors. But lead us not into temptation, but deliver us from evil. For thine is the kingdom, and the power, and the glory, forever. Amen." She told me that any time I pray, to hold up my prayer beside this perfect prayer, and I will always be okay. After praying this prayer that night, she had total peace. Her worry went away. She enacted her faith, which is believing God's word is true no matter what your circumstances seem to be.

Can you do things that God cannot?

_____

If God has let go of your sin, then how can you still hold on to it?

_____

_____

_____

_____

It would be like a man being released from prison, but refusing to go. When you hold on to your sin after God has let it go, what message are you sending Him? You are in essence telling Him that sending His son to die on the cross was not enough to forgive you of your sin. You are telling Him your sin is too great for His sacrifice to cover. You are trying to be mightier than God. Now I know that might seem a little harsh. I know you never consciously set out to tell God all these things. But not believing or putting into practice what His Word says is just continuing on the path God never intended for you. When you do this, you are never allowing yourself to live fully in the present because of the hold you keep on yourself from the past. How do you think this affects your daily life? Write your answer on the next page:

> *It's not whether you get knocked down, it's whether you get up again.*
> Vince Lombardi

_____

_____

_____

How do you think this affects your present relationships?

_____

_____

_____

Are you ready to pray? I have written out a prayer below. Pray it out loud with the boldness and authority of someone ready to start a new life:

Dear Heavenly Father,

I praise you and thank you, Lord! You have given me so much, and for that I am so grateful. I want to ask You right now Lord to hear my prayer. This is one of the most important prayers I have ever prayed in my life, and I don't want anything to stand in the way of Your hearing it, so please wipe away any sin in my life. I want to be spotless before You. Lord I want only Your will for my life. I know that you created me in Your image. Your image does not include all the baggage that came with my abortion. I am ready to lay this baggage down. I have been mentally and physically drained at times from carrying it around, and I now know that that is not your will for my life. Lord, I want my life to reflect your will as it is in heaven. I want to walk as closely to you here on this earth as I physically can. Lord, I will trust you daily. Please help me when I start to worry about the past or when I don't "feel" forgiven. Remind me to enact my faith. Let me have the peace of knowing that it doesn't matter how I feel. My faith and Your word tell me I *am* forgiven. I have learned if You have forgiven me, I can no longer hold on to this pain. Deliver me from it forever, Lord. I lay it down once and for all, never to pick it up again. The pain, shame, sorrows, and regret I have felt from the choice of abortion no longer have a hold on me. Thank you, Lord Jesus, for giving me the boldness and authority I needed to pray this prayer. I will forever love you and praise your name!

In Jesus's name I pray, Amen.

Read **Isaiah 44:22**.

The word *redeemed* in *Webster's* is defined as follows:

1. To set free, rescue or ransom.
2. To save from a state of sinfulness and its consequences.

That's what you are—redeemed! You have been set free, you have been rescued, you have been saved from a state of sinfulness *and* its consequences!

> *God's love has taken off my chains, and given me these wings.*
> **Steven Curtis Chapman**

What did this section teach you about forgiveness?

_____

_____

_____

What steps can you take this week to put this knowledge into practice?

_____

_____

_____

Read **Psalm 30** to close out this chapter.

Write your memory verse for the week:

_____

_____

_____

> *I am free.*
> **"Penny,"**
> **in SaveOne**
> **class**

Please use the journal pages that follow to write about your feelings and what this chapter has meant to you.

Journal Page

Journal Page

Journal Page

Journal Page

Journal Page

Chapter Eight:
Renewing Your Mind

Verse to memorize this week: *Don't copy the behavior and customs of this world, but let God transform you into a new person by changing the way you think. Then you will know what God wants you to do, and you will know how good and pleasing and perfect His will really is.*
Romans 12:2 NLT

hen you renew your mind, you think differently about your problems. When you don't renew your mind, Satan has a playground to torment you. Satan will bombard you with wrong thinking as much as you will let him. I am here to tell you; *you don't have to let him!* Renewing your mind is simply training it to believe and think only the thoughts that line up with the Word of God. Satan is a liar. Read John 8:44. Jesus tells us ". . . there is no truth in him."

> *The mind of man is the battleground on which every moral and spiritual battle is fought.*
> **J. Oswald Sanders**

Let's look at some thoughts you might have or have had, and see if they line up with scripture. In the blank provided, write *S* if the thought is from Satan; *G* if the thought lines up with the word of God:

"I need to remind myself of my abortion, that way I will honor the memory of my child."

_____

Read **Philippians 4:8**.

"I am a horrible person, what kind of person would have an abortion?"

_____

Read **Colossians 3:10**.

"It's okay to talk about my abortion because I'm forgiven."

_____

Read **John 8:36**.

"I don't deserve to be forgiven."

_____

Read **Romans 3:23**.

"I need to think about my child, and one day seeing him/her again. What a wonderful day that will be!"

_____

Read **Philippians 4:8**.

∾❀∾

Read **John 10:10**.
Satan came to kill, steal, and destroy. He has stolen enough of your life away by keeping the shame of your abortion at the forefront of your mind. Read the second part of that verse again. Jesus came so you will have life and have it more abundantly. It is time to reclaim the years Satan has stolen from you by renewing your mind. Decide right now that you will not allow him to steal any more time from your life. Speak to him and confess it out loud. He can't see your thoughts like Christ can, but He can certainly hear you. Do that now in your own words, and then write down what you said to Him:

_____

_____

_____

_____

_____

_____

_____

Write **Philippians 4:8**:

_____

_____

These are the things we should be thinking about. When you have a thought that twists your mind, you need to hold it up and ask yourself, Is this pure? Is this noble? Is this a good report? Is this a lovely thought? If it is not, then bring it into captivity.

Read **2 Corinthians 10:4–5**.
What is a stronghold?

_____

_____

_____

Where do our weapons come from, according to this scripture?

_____

_____

What does this scripture mean when it says we are to cast down any high thing that exalts itself against the knowledge of God?

_____

_____

_____

> *Our defeat or victory begins with what we think, and if we guard our thoughts we shall not have much trouble anywhere else along the line.*
> **Vance Havner**

107

What are we supposed to do with our thoughts?

_____

_____

How do we bring our thoughts into captivity to the obedience of Christ?

_____

_____

_____

When, not *if*, Satan throws these darts at you, reminding you of your past, you need to have a plan of action to conquer him. When you accomplish something grand, like what you are doing right now by allowing God to heal your past, Satan will do all he can to try to tell you it wasn't real. He will throw these darts at your most vulnerable areas.

❧

Read **Matthew 9:17**.
How can you relate this verse to your mind?

_____

_____

_____

You can't have a new life with an old way of thinking. Set a new standard for yourself and your future. You don't have to accept past defeats. You have the opportunity right now to break the negative cycle in your life. Get rid of the old wineskin and get ready for God to change your life.

❧

Let me tell you a story of one girl who came to one of my SaveOne classes. I recognized her immediately as the lady I had seen pushing her son around church in his wheelchair. The first night she couldn't speak, she was crying so hard. During introductions as part of the discussion, she was able to get out her name, but that was it. The following week she came back and proceeded to tell us her story. She had had an abortion years before and then later, after marriage, she became pregnant again. She gave birth to a son who had cerebral palsy. She believed from that point on she never could tell anyone of her abortion. Her fear was that everyone would look at her son in his wheelchair and believe that was God's condemnation on her life. When she said this in class, the realization of just how despicable Satan is became clear to me. He will stop at nothing. If he will take the most innocent of creation, a handicapped child, and use that against his own mother there is no telling what he will do.

> *You cannot stay where you are and go with God.*
> **Blackaby and King, Experiencing God**

My friend, Donna, has come so far since that night. She finished the class and was able to drive out that lie Satan made her believe for so long. She now teaches our SaveOne classes and is able to talk about her past without any condemnation.

The key is, she renewed her mind. She allowed God to make her thinking new. She held up that lie from Satan against the word of God and realized it simply was not true. Satan will finally leave you alone when you become stronger and he realizes this is not a vulnerable area for you any longer.

Another thing my pastor has told me is, "Confessing the word of God by faith corrects my mental picture." When you think wrong thoughts, have a counterthought ready. Look back on those statements at the beginning of this chapter. You may also want to look at the shame statements from chapter four. What is a counterthought that lines up with the Word of God for each of the statements that are from Satan? Write them in the following blanks:

Example

Shame statement: "I'm worthless."

Positive confession: "I am created in the image of God, therefore I have great worth in the eyes of God!"

_____

_____

_____

_____

_____

_____

_____

_____

_____

_____

_____

_____

_____

_____

_____

_____

_____

_____

_____

Learn these statements, then as Satan throws the darts, you will have a positive confession from the Word of God to fight them. State them out loud at each occurrence. That will be your confession, further correcting your mental picture.

You might say to me, "Sheila, how do you expect me to have a good mental picture after all I've been through?"

Maybe, by looking at my picture on the cover of this book, you assume I've got it all together and that I've always had this great life. Let me tell you, that hasn't always been the case. I've made many bad choices that resulted in horrific consequences such as a past rape, my abortion, drug abuse, and alcohol abuse. Before that I suffered some horrific consequences because of other bad decisions that had nothing to do with me, such as sexual, physical, and mental abuse as a child. I know a lot of times, not always, an abortion is just a furtherance of a pattern of abuse throughout a person's life. But I can tell you from experience, your life doesn't have to continue on this path. Now because of my good choices, I bring about good consequences, resulting in a positive life. You no longer have to be a victim. Turn your will toward God and allow him to work.

> *Every temptation comes to us via our thoughts.*
> **Erwin Lutzer, *Those Sins that Won't Budge***

One of my favorite songs is from the CD *Refresh* by Dan Smith. The name of it is "*I Surrender All.*" One line of that song says, "Take my will and mold it in your pleasure." By allowing your past and whatever may be there to dictate your future and your thoughts is tying God's hands. You're not allowing Him to do a great work in you. You need to let Him take your will and mold it as He pleases.

Read **Philippians 1:6.**

God is trying to do a great work in you. But He will not go against your will. You have to renew your mind and stop allowing your past to make you think negatively. Negative thoughts create a negative person.

Read **Proverbs 23:7**.
What you think, you will be. If you think of yourself as a victim, then that is all you will ever be. You will never taste the sweet victory God has for you. Allow God to take your past and whatever may be in it and turn it into His mighty tool to help others.

> *You cannot have a positive life and a negative mind.*
>
> **Joyce Meyer,**
> **Battlefield of**
> **the Mind**

Read **Psalm 119:93**.
My Bible uses the word *precepts* in this verse, which means a particular course of action. In essence this verse is saying, "to never forget Gods course of action He gives you, because by this He has given you life."

Where can you find God's course of action?

I hope your answer was *the Bible*. This is where you find all your answers. This is where the basis for renewing your mind will always come from. This is where you need to be to get God's word implanted deep inside you for future reference. Don't let this be the end of your study. You have developed the habit of studying, looking up scripture, and memorizing scripture over these past few weeks. Don't let this study be the end. Continue on after you have finished this book. You will find the renewal process so much more pleasant than the alternative.

Seeds have been planted in your mind that need time to grow. Don't give up. Renewing your mind is a process. It's not something that is going to happen overnight and then "keep." Renewing your mind is a lifelong journey that is a marvelous journey.

Renewing Your Mind

What did this section teach you about the renewal of your mind?

_____

_____

_____

What steps can you take this week to put this knowledge into practice?

_____

_____

_____

Write your memory verse for the week:

_____

_____

_____

Journal Page

Journal Page

Chapter Nine:
Who Is This Child?

Verse to memorize this week: *Let us draw near with a true heart in full assurance of faith, having our hearts sprinkled from an evil conscience and our bodies washed with pure water. Without wavering, let us hold tightly to the hope we say we have, for God can be trusted to keep his promise.* **Hebrews 10:22–23 NLT**

This course you are taking is about life, reclaiming your own life as well as your child's. Through the work you will do in this chapter, you will bestow the dignity and honor on your child he/she so deserves. When your child's soul was ushered into heaven, he/she became part of a nameless, faceless sea of statistics. This is your opportunity to change all that.

Have you ever allowed yourself to think about your child? Have you ever wondered if your child was a boy or girl? Have you ever wondered what he/she looks like? Don't be afraid to think these thoughts. I know there will be pain involved in finding the answers to these questions. But Christ is still here with you.

> *She became a real person to me. It was like instead of nine months and delivering a baby, I spent twelve weeks working through the past and delivering a fifteen-year-old daughter. She is so real to me now.* **"Ann," in SaveOne class**

Read **Deuteronomy 31:6, 8.**
What two things will God not do?

He was with you when you started this book, and He is still here now. He is intimately involved in every detail of your life. Please take a moment and say a prayer asking God to give you His peace and comfort that goes above and beyond our human comprehension (**Philippians 4:7**) as you work through this chapter.

One of the most common uncertainties you might have is whether your child was a boy or a girl. You might believe this is a question you will never know until you reach heaven, but this is simply not true. You don't have to accept this uncertainty and remain in the dark. Christ knows the answer to your question. He will tell you if you ask. He has always known your child. **Jeremiah 1:5** says, "Before I formed you in the womb I knew you . . . " He is right there in heaven with him or her. As hard as this might be, I want you to put down this book right now and take as long as you need. Talk to God; tell Him you have remained in the dark long enough. Tell Him you are ready to give this child life. Then ask Him to reveal to you the gender of your child.

Finish this sentence: My child is a _____.

Do you believe your child is in heaven? Why or why not?

_____

_____

_____

2 Corinthians 5:8 in the New Living Translation says, *"Yes, we are fully confident, and we would rather be away from these bodies, for then we will be at home with the Lord."*

To be absent from your body is to be present with Christ. Your child never got to experience life here on this earth. Therefore he/she never had the opportunity to sin or develop any bad habits that would keep him/her out of heaven. When your child's soul left your body, it was pure, blameless, and spotless before the Lord.

Who Is This Child?

Now that you know if your child was a boy or girl, I want you to think for a moment about his/her physical characteristics. Would she be tall? Would he have curly hair? Would she be musical? Would he love baseball? Write in detail what you believe your child's appearance and personality would be:

_____

_____

_____

_____

_____

_____

_____

_____

_____

Are you starting to see your child? Can you picture him/ her in heaven? What do you think life is like for him/her in heaven?

_____

_____

_____

_____

_____

_____

You now have an image of your child. You might have seen her running the bases. You might be picturing him riding a bike. Whatever your mind sees of your child, whether it's a tiny baby, or a grown woman, this person in heaven needs a name. Naming your child will give you a great sense of identification with your child. It will be one more step in giving your child life, as well as recognizing him/her as a human being worthy of a name. This name is what plucks your child out of that sea of nameless, faceless statistics and makes him/her stand tall and proud. Again, take some time for uninterrupted prayer. Name your child. Write name(s) below:

_____

_____

_____

At times, I imagine I see your face in the wind, in a beautiful sunset, or when I look into a rainbow. I see us walking hand in hand, with your beautiful blond curls about your face, and eyes as beautiful as the sky. When I come back to reality, I know that when I enter Heaven's gates, you will be there to meet me and we will walk hand in hand.
"Joni,"
excerpt from letter to child

Read **Revelation 21:4**.
What four things does it say will be no more?

_____

_____

_____

_____

How can these four things be no more?

_____

_____

_____

If you had an opportunity to talk with your child, what would you say? On the following page, write a letter to your child. Tell him/her all the things you would like to say, but never got the chance:

Who Is This Child?

Dear

There is one more thing I want you to do. Giving your child a place of honor within your home is another exercise in bestowing dignity. Creating a memorial will bring your child into his/her rightful place in your family. This doesn't have to be anything huge. My memorial to my daughter Meghan is simply a pink candle in a tulip candleholder. It sits in the middle of a table full of family photos. I don't have a picture of my daughter, but I can place the memorial for her alongside the pictures of the other people I love. Just to give you a few examples, we have had women do everything from being extremely creative and painting a mural on her wall, to planting gardens, to buying a tiny teddy bear to sit on her nightstand. Make this memorial fit your talents and likes. This memorial also doesn't have to be anything you have to explain to people who come to your home. No one ever asks about the candle; it just looks like something I've put there for decoration. Also, you don't have to have this completed before you finish this class. But I would like for you to have an idea and know what you are going to accomplish. Another nice thing is to share it with the class if you feel comfortable doing that. When you tell each other about your memorials, it's always fun and a very special time together when you see each other's talents and creativity.

Write out some ideas for your memorial. Or if you know already what you're going to do, write it below:

_____

_____

_____

_____

_____

Who Is This Child?

What if your child could talk to you? I want to share with you a letter that a lady going through the SaveOne class wrote. I think it is a fantastic mental picture of what heaven is like for your child and what he/she would say to you if he/she could:

Dear Mom,

Just want you to know everything is fine. I'm sitting here in my usual place, resting in the arms of Dad. Dad told me about your secret pain you have been carrying around for so many years of your earthly life. I don't quite understand what pain is, because here there is none. I don't quite understand what years are, because here there is no time.

Dad told me it was hard for you to ask my brother, Jesus, for forgiveness. I asked Jesus what you needed this "forgiveness" for. He said He didn't remember exactly what you did. He said something about the "sea of forgetfulness" is why He couldn't remember. He said He had this forgiveness for you even before you were born and that He was just waiting for your heart to take it.

He told me He lived for a while where you are now so He could make a way for you to come home. I asked Dad about the place you live. It sounds so different than here. He said He loves giving all His kids where you are presents. I have been noticing though that some kids don't like His presents, or they simply don't care to ask. He said it was because they were prideful and embarrassed. Those are awfully big words that I just don't understand. I asked Him, Why does He keep giving presents to kids who don't want them? He said because the kids all belong to Him, and He wants to bring all of them home. He said He loves them no matter what. That I understand.

There are a lot of kids here, Mom, that are just like me; just like there are a lot of Moms where you are just like you.

I asked Dad why you and me are apart from one another. He said He wanted to show the world His miracles, so He put you where you are to let everyone see what a miracle is. I think He called you His daughter of Amazing Grace, a child of His unconditional love. I guess you know by now Dad uses some

Until now you have been a nameless, faceless part of my past. But tonight, I give you life by giving you a name and publicly acknowledging your presence in my life. God ushered you into His midst, an angel unforgotten, and it is with Him you will remain. While it has taken ten years for me to learn that I could love you, I promise that now I will never stop.

"Bobbie,"
excerpt from
letter to child

125

pretty big words. Boy, when He speaks, things really happen!

I want you to know, Mama, that I'll always and forever love you because always and forever is what love is . . . and Mama, one last thing. I just want to say thanks for giving me a name to sign this letter.

Love,
Your daughter,
Rachel Grace

What did this section teach you about your child?

_____

_____

_____

_____

What steps can you take this week to put this knowledge into practice?

_____

_____

_____

_____

Write your memory verse for the week:

_____

_____

_____

Journal Page

Journal Page

Journal Page

Journal Page

Chapter Ten:
A Woman of Courage

Verse to memorize this week: *For God hath not given us the spirit of fear; but of power, and of love, and of a sound mind.* **2 Timothy 1:7**.

I was sitting in church one Sunday listening to my pastor. He was preaching a sermon entitled "Giants of the Bible." One of those giants was a lady named Esther, who I had long admired and studied. At that time I had just been writing this book for a few weeks and thought I had an idea for all the chapters that would be included. Suddenly, the title of this chapter popped into my head. I knew how I had admired the courage of each woman that works through this class, but I understood that you may not realize the magnitude of what you have just accomplished and how it can be used.

Work through this chapter, and let each story and each scripture sink in. Let what you learn through this chapter develop a steely resolve in your heart; and make a determination that you will never go back to the bondage you started out with some twelve weeks ago. Let's begin with the story of Esther and learn more of why she is one of our "giants" of the Bible.

Esther was a Jewish orphan, raised by her Uncle Mordecai. He had a strong faith, and he made sure that faith was instilled in her. They were part of a huge group of Jewish people living in Persia. They are considered captives, the spoils of war. God's heart remains forever attached to this group; they are His chosen people! One day the king of Persia divorces his wife and goes on a hunt to find a new queen. He appointed men from each of the 127 provinces of his kingdom to gather up the prettiest virgin women and

> *Courage is that quality of mind which enables men to encounter danger or difficulty with firmness, or without fear or depression of spirits... The highest degree of courage is seen in the person who is most fearful but refuses to capitulate to it.*
>
> **J. Oswald Sanders**

bring them to his palace. He even said to give them some make-up! Can you imagine this happening today? Okay, let's get on with the story so you can understand how Esther came to be known as such a remarkable, courageous lady.

After all these ladies had been gathered, they spent twelve months readying themselves for the king. Esther was among those taken from her home, and forced to participate in this "beauty pageant" with untold amounts of other ladies. The scriptures explain her as being, "beautiful in form and lovely to look at." Mordecai had instructed her before she was taken to never divulge that she was a Jew. She kept that promise to him and it paid off. She endured the beauty pageant and actually won the heart of the king. He took her into his palace and gave her the crown.

Now, let's switch to Uncle Mordecai. He was always hanging around the king's gate. While out there one day, he heard of an evil plot from these two men. Their plan was to kill the king. When Mordecai heard of this, he got word to Esther and she informed the king in Mordecai's name. They found this plot to be true. Immediately, those two men were hanged, and the king's life was saved. After this the king took a man named Haman and promoted him to be his right-hand man.

Now, you might be thinking, How unfair! Well, it was. Life is not always fair. But the scripture doesn't say Mordecai started ranting and raving because the king hadn't even honored him for saving his life. He stayed steady and firm and did not relent in his beliefs. He didn't have to defend himself; he knew God would do the defending for him. When God is on your side, what more do you need?

Now that Haman had been promoted, everyone had to bow down to him and pay honor. This flew in the face of everything Mordecai knew to be true. He would not bow down to anyone but God. When Mordecai refused it made Haman furious. Because of Mordecai's refusal, Haman decided he would not only kill him, but kill all his people as well. He was going to destroy every Jew living in the kingdom. Haman went to the king and told him what he was going to do. The king gave him his blessing and said, "Do with them as you please."

So Haman went full steam ahead. When Mordecai learned of Haman's plan, he was absolutely heartbroken. He sent word to Esther about what was going on, and now she was agonizing as well. Mordecai also asked her to go to the king and beg mercy for the Jewish people. Esther informed her uncle that it was a law that no person could go to the king unless summoned. If you did, you would be put to death.

Read **Esther 4:13–14**.
I believe this passage of scripture is the most defining in the entire book of Esther. She could remain silent and just be the status quo, and help for the Jews would come from some other source, or she could realize this might be her calling. God could have made her to have attained her royal position for this, her finest hour. Mordecai is telling her in this passage to Stand! Speak! Die! But whatever she does, do not remain silent. Read her response to her uncle, in **Esther 4:16**.

What a woman of courage. She knew from where her strength had to come. Not from her own royal position or her beauty, which got her there in the first place. But because of her calling for the fast, she knew her strength and courage had to come from only one place: God. She knew it was a great possibility she would perish in this endeavor, but it was worth it to her to try to save these innocent people.

After three days had passed, she asked the king and Haman to a banquet she was preparing in their honor. The king was excited, and he and Haman attended the banquet. While at the banquet, the king asked what the occasion was. All Esther told him was that she wanted him to come to another banquet she was preparing for him and Haman the next day.

Haman left there happy, and went outside where he ran into Mordecai. Mordecai just sat there. He didn't jump up, bow down, or show respect of any kind to Haman. Again, that infuriated Haman. So he went and had a fifty-foot gallows made on which to hang Mordecai.

Why should I fear? I am on a Royal Mission. I am in the service of the King of Kings.

Mary Slessor, beginning her remarkable missionary career in Calabar (now part of modern Nigeria)

While the gallows was being made for Mordecai, the king was inside, unable to sleep. He sent for the record book of his kingdom, and was reminded of the account when the two men were going to kill him and Mordecai had saved his life. He asked what was ever done for him, and his servants said, "Nothing." The king then called for Haman, who just happened to be on his way to tell him about his great plan to hang Mordecai on the gallows he just had built. The king started asking him what he could do for someone he wants to honor. Of course, Haman just assumed the king wanted to honor him! So he started telling the king all the things HE would love. He requested a royal robe that had been worn by the king and a royal horse ridden by the king, and then let him be led around on this horse by a great man in the kingdom for all the people in the town to admire.

After hearing all this, the king told Haman that it was a great idea, and he told him to do all this for Mordecai. Imagine the look of shock and disbelief on Haman's face. How funny would that have been? Haman had to go and complete this humiliating task for Mordecai.

I love Mordecai and his attitude, because the scripture says, afterward, he just went back to the king's gate to wait. Haman, on the other hand, hurried home with his head in his hands, embarrassed and totally disgraced.

A Woman of Courage

Read **Esther 7:1–4.**

Can you believe the way she was able to hold it together? She's begging for her life and the lives of every Jew living in Persia. Every bit of their future rests squarely on her shoulders at this moment. But yet she knew her God was able to do what she could not. She drew on a well of tremendous courage that did not come from herself, but from God.

The king automatically wanted to know who devised this plan to kill the Jews. Haman was singled out. He also was told of the fifty-foot gallows that had been built to hang Mordecai. The king was enraged and commanded Haman be hung on his own gallows.

Is this irony or what? The very plan Haman was preparing ended up being used against him. That is probably an outcome Esther never imagined. God didn't tell her up front what was going to happen. If He had, would that have taken any courage on Esther's part? No, she could have breezed through the banquets, and probably wouldn't have fasted. Instead, she took the whole ordeal very seriously and did what God told her to do. The outcome was what God wanted. You can continue to read in Esther what happened to the Jewish people. I will tell you, this story has a very happy ending.

Write your memory verse for the week:

_____

_____

_____

This verse certainly describes Esther, doesn't it? But who else does it describe? Do you believe it describes you? Why or why not?

_____

_____

_____

The word *power* could be translated into the word *courage*. Do you believe you have a spirit of courage? Why or why not?

_____

_____

God also gave you a sound mind. Do you believe because of your courage to take this course your mind is more sound? Why or why not?

_____

_____

_____

Where did Esther get such courage?

_____

In one part of the story, Esther is told that if she does not become the person to save the Jews that help will arise from another place. What do you believe would have happened to Esther if she had shrunk into the background and refused to help?

_____

_____

That certainly would have been easier wouldn't it? After all, she was the queen. She had servants at her beck and call. She had everything in life she would ever desire. But she also had strong beliefs, an unshakable faith, and tremendous courage.

My abortion is no longer a secret. It is a mighty tool in the hands of a mighty God.
"Jennifer," in SaveOne class

Read **Psalm 121.**

Take each verse and, starting on the next page write in your own words what we're told about God and how He keeps us.

A Woman of Courage

Verse 1:

_____

_____

_____

Verse 2:

_____

_____

_____

Verse 3:

_____

_____

_____

Verse 4:

_____

_____

_____

Verse 5:

_____

_____

_____

Verse 6:

_____

_____

_____

Verse 7:

_____

_____

_____

Verse 8:

_____

_____

_____

If we truly believe what this Psalm says, we will have the courage to do whatever God asks of us. We have to believe it though and put that belief into practice. Esther is a great example of someone who tested the scriptures to see if they hold true. By her accomplishing what she did, she paved the way for us to follow. We follow her through learning from her experiences. By her actions, she made it easier for us to believe we can accomplish the same things.

Throughout history, studies had been performed and research conducted to conclude that man could not break the four-minute mark in the mile run. Experts told us it was a human impossibility to run a mile that fast. Along came Roger Bannister. He did not allow the studies, the research, or the scientists to convince him he couldn't run that fast.

He then became the first man ever to break the four-minute mile.

Do you think Bannister just woke up one day and decided to break that record? No, he trained, relentlessly, for that day. But guess what has happened since Roger Bannister achieved his goal? More than three hundred people broke that same record after he paved the way. There were mental barriers that kept runners from believing they could ever achieve this record. But this one man set a new standard just because he believed he could. By his accomplishment, he broke down the mental barriers that stood in the way.

What courage that must have taken for this man to shun "fact" and believe he could do more. He found out that the impossibility to run a four-minute mile was really not a fact at all.

Regarding your abortion experience, name something you believed to be fact, and now realize it is not:

_____

_____

_____

Read **Luke 18:43.**
What happened to the blind man?

_____

_____

Do you feel as though this is what has happened to you?

_____

What took place when everyone saw the miracle Jesus performed?

_____

_____

> God is directing us not to make the past a port or an anchor when the wind is still blowing fresh breezes for our future direction.
>
> **Pastor Maury Davis, Cornerstone Church**

> I want to help others to have complete healing. No matter if it is one, two, or more. That sea of forgetfulness is big enough for them all.
>
> **"Linda,"** in SaveOne class

139

What do you think would have happened if the man receiving his sight simply went into his home and told no one what Christ had done for him?

_____

_____

It is only natural for you to want to tell others when something good happens. It's not always so easy when that something good involves being released from emotional bondage and the affects of a past abortion. This is when we have to draw from our source of courage. What is our source of courage?

_____

_____

You may not have a desire to join us at SaveOne and start speaking in front of large audiences. We also don't suggest casually telling your co-workers or family about your past. You have gone through some mighty changes, that doesn't mean all the people around you have also. Allow God to use you when the time is right. I can't explain it, but it seems as though God steers the people to you who need to hear what He has done. We get calls all the time from women who have finished this book who tell us about being faced with the issue of abortion and being able to talk intelligently. Their old response would have been to run to the bathroom and cry or be extremely embarrassed. What we have found is the woman that finishes this book goes back to her workplace or home and becomes the wife, mother, friend, or sister she was meant to be without all the emotional baggage.

Write **Psalm 30:6**:

_____

_____

_____

The New Living Translation of this verse says, *"Nothing will stop me now!"* You have to have an unwavering determination that you will not be stopped. Don't *ever* let Satan turn you back into a victim. *You are a victor!* Promise yourself that you will not look back, that you will always look ahead.

Read **Isaiah 43:18–19**.
What does verse **18** tell you to forget?

_____

_____

_____

> The devil will give up when he sees you are not going to give in.
> **Joyce Meyer, Battlefield of the Mind**

What does verse **19** tell you God will do for you?

_____

_____

_____

Read **Ephesians 6:12–20**.
Have a plan ready for when, not if, Satan attacks your mind and tries to make you remember the lies you believed for so long. This is a battle you are in for your mind. Be immovable, and believe that he will never win that battle again. Write out your plan of action to guard your mind against attack:

_____

_____

_____

Read **Philippians 1:6**.
Don't let this be the end of the story. Continue on this journey of drawing closer to God and developing a deeper relationship with Him. Believe that God has started a work in you and will follow it to completion throughout your life.

I have one last bit of homework for you that is actually a challenge. My challenge to you is to SaveOne. Think of one person you know who has been hurt by the effects of abortion. After preparing yourself through much prayer, draw from your source of courage and work to assimilate him/her (yes, we have had men go through this class, too) into a SaveOne class. They may tell you no, and that's all right. God will do the rest. He will get the glory from your effort and your courage to step out and tell your story.

Remember . . . Esther already paved the way.

Write your memory verse for the week:

_____

_____

_____

No, dear brothers and sisters, I am still not all I should be, but I am focusing all my energies on this one thing: Forgetting the past and looking forward to what lies ahead, I strain to reach the end of the race and receive the prize for which God, through Christ Jesus, is calling us up to heaven.

Philippians 3:13–14.

> *We are here to teach tomorrow's children through our experience, and God's merciful Grace. We are the missing arms of love, the missing voice of truth. It doesn't matter when we learned it or how long it took us to get to the place of today. Tomorrow's children are on their way here.*
> **"Brandi,"**
> **in SaveOne**
> **class**

Journal Page

Journal Page

Journal Page

In Conclusion

Don't let this journey end here. Use the knowledge God has given you through this study to help others.

Please contact our office, and we will assist you in every way to help transform the lives of those who have been ravaged by abortion.

SaveOne—help for men and women who are suffering in silence after abortion.

Be the willing vessel who will start a chapter of SaveOne in your area.

www.saveone.org
866-329-3571
info@saveone.org

CPSIA information can be obtained
at www.ICGtesting.com
Printed in the USA
LVOW11s0725061216
515964LV00001B/1/P